On The Religious Objections To The Use Of Chloroform

De Quincey, Francis John

Francis John de Quincey

On the

Religious Objections

to the use of

Chloroform in Obstetric Medicine.

By

Francis John de Quincey.

31st March, 1849.

b.

Sir Philip. "Look at the summits of all the trees around us, how they move! And the loftiest the most so. Nothing is at rest within the compass of our view but the grey moss upon the Park Pales. Let that moss eat away the dead oak; but let it not be compared with the living one."

From a Conversation between Sir Philip Sidney & Lord Brooke.

4.

Nothing is more calculated to diminish our good opinion of the probity and disinterestedness of our fellow man, than taking a glance at the history of inventions and discoveries. The fate of nearly every originator has been that of Prometheus in the ancient story: and few indeed have been the inheritors of genius who have not also been compelled to endure the vulture and the rock.

Excepting for the purpose of illustration, there is little need to recur at any length to the history that has preceded the full establishment and recognition of our brightest and most highly valued achievements. In truth it has been in all ages the same in its intimate nature; however the changed spirit of the time, or the circumstances of each particular case, may have altered its external manifestations. For although people raise their voices against the imprisonment of Galileo and the persecution of the Lollards, we, in our own time and in our own country, perceive men engaged in the same work of detraction, exhibiting the same spirit of malevolence and calling to their aid the same antiquated system of prejudice and of bigotry; for the like purpose of crushing those who are seeking after truth and endeavouring to do good.

The two great discoveries in medical science by men now living, namely the reflex theory of Marshall Hall and the theory of Cytogenesis of Schwann, Schleiden and Goodsir, furnish excellent examples of the truth of this opinion. And in the yet nascent discovery of the application of Chloroform to Anaesthetic purposes the same course has been pursued.

However consoling it may be to reflect that Harvey, Jenner, Mascagni, Bell, Hunter and Paré, and the bearer of every name illustrious in the records of our profession,

have endured the same fate; in like
manner have had to war against
prejudice and against ignorance; and
that the ultimate glory of each has
always been proportional to his early
antagonism: and although it is
equally consoling to think that the
discovery of printing and the increasing
enlightenment of the world have
placed it out of the power of any
set of men permanently and
successfully to combat novelty, or to
prevent new ideas from spreading
as their merits may deserve :— it
is not the less to be regretted that
there still exists a large class of
mankind, who considering the
words old and good as synonymous,
can admire nothing that has not
upon it the dust of forty generations;
and to whom novelty is a mere rock
of offence. And such constitute one of the two classes
that oppose chloroform. Far be it from me to
depreciate the caution which naturally
and properly exists, as reg'r to the

admission of new theories into medicine as into other sciences. What I would object to is the rejection of facts, illustrated and supported by daily experience; from attachment to an ancient opinion, as in the case of the reflex theory; or on account of a fanciful interpretation of a divine sentence, as witnessed in the history of chloroform.

But while we can only regret the existence of such a class as I have now spoken of; and while we may still be permitted to respect them, as holding their opinions in sincerity, though in error, there is another for whom I confess myself to have neither sympathy nor respect. And within this body are to be found the most violent opponents of chloroform. Under the mask of moral or physical objections, they entertain a secret but deeply rooted prejudice against every thing that they have no concern.

But such surely mistake the objects of man's life. They are broadly declared to be two: to do good and to discover truth. And these are set forth as the end of all mens' lives: not of a sept or country. We ought then to possess a Catholic spirit towards the good and the truth, no matter whence it may come.

As those of whom I speak are unable to fulfil the latter of these objects, so they appear unwilling to perform the former. And thus they pass through life; detraction and opposition their sole offering to others who are able and disposed to do both. To recur to the Promethean fable the world is their rock on which they would bind the man of genius; their own ambition being to enact the part of the vulture, and gnawing at his vitals, to deprive him of his heaven derived power, of speaking directly to the souls of men.

There is in Medicine, as
in all other sciences whose outer
boundary is beyond the circle of
what is exact or physical, an eminent
necessity for perfect freedom from
prejudice and for dispassionate
consideration. It has now reached a
point in its progress when many
discoveries may be looked which can
not be clearly and incontrovertibly
demonstrated to our senses; when more
must be acknowleged as established
by reasoning processes than can actually
become visible to our eyes. As members,
then, of a liberal profession, it is absolutely
incumbent on us to examine scrupulously
for ourselves the arguments as well as
the facts which lead to a particular
line of practice: and while we are
called upon to decline the adoption
of ill supported and unnecessary
hypotheses, we are equally bound
imperatively to take our stand by
that which our judgement ——— mends.
Not adopting the ——— ———

station we claim. We do not perform its
duties and consequently we are unworthy
of its privileges. We do not attend to the sacred
duty which the very nature of our Profession
imposes on us and which ought to constrain
us to adopt every safe and possible means
within our reach to relieve suffering and
to shorten disease. Every profession has its
requirements: this is the vitally important
one demanded at our hands.

    In such a world of progress as
this, the study of existing facts, though
vastly important, is not all it is our duty
to attend to: ~~the case of~~ our memory
and our faculties of observation, though
of gigantic use, do not complete the
circle of our mental endowments.
The use of our reasoning powers, as
men, must aid us, as medical practitioners,
in calling into question and deciding
upon the relative claims of discoverers
and their opponents. We must weigh
the arguments on both sides, if there
be arguments on both sides, and a
verdict well and truly give according

to the evidence which is before us.

And hitherto has this been the course pursued? Have discoverers received due honor in our profession? Have their improvements been adopted readily and their merits recognized and rewarded? Has merit been the sole criterion by which we have been guided in our decision?

To each and all of these questions a simple two and for historical truth compels us to reply in the negative. The history of the progress of medicine unveils a sad tale to the contrary: Exhibits a dark picture of ideas good and excellent in themselves combatted unworthily by bigotry or by simple absurdity.

Even in this age, as I said before, we find the old spirit existing among a large body who are nominally allied with us in prosecuting the Medical profession; Although the one it is to see that a are than before: an. A field i will have a more harmless use now than as the sites for burning those unhappy beings who disagree in their opinions with the majority of their neighbours. But But still the spirit that is abroad is the same. And while, as is expressed in my motto, all the world around us is changing, there are yet to be found men who are willing to represent the grey moss upon the dark pales and are desirous of crushing the life out of the living oak. There are dead ones enough encumbering our steps, and if they would be content with preying upon such all would be well. But they desire to lay hands upon the living, breathing and yearning being who is to carry on the good work, to achieve new victories and to gain new light.

My chief reason for writing this thesis is to protest against these people.

~~and before me, ... his right~~
~~by radical ... that the better~~
~~... power~~

Before passing to the more
immediate subject of my thesis it may then
be well to take a brief glance at the
history of the more important innovations
into Medical Science: from which we
may draw some useful and practical
conclusions in relation to the question
to be afterwards discussed; as well as
in regard to the general principles
which ought to guide us in the
investigations and inquiries ~~which~~
that at various times it will be our
duty to make. For this is an age of
discoveries; and we have much reason
to believe that with the means of research
we now possess our science will rapidly
advance! This must ever be done
by the progressive enlightenment and
development the Almighty has granted
us suggesting, deviations from the
old paths of error. Man's soul
has too great an affinity with its Maker

to strong a desire to strike into being the
eternal spark that shall slay death,
to suffer ignorance to continue longer
than it can help. He is feverish and
restless, every moment the dull
hollow sound of the earth flung upon
his coffin seems to moan in his ears,
and he is agony haunted until he
uprears a great thought: then comes
another and another that in the
universal movement join. And it
it is no answer to this opinion to say with
Mr Park of Liverpool "that we have done
very well without improvements, and may
do very well again and therefore they are
not to be adopted". For this is untrue, seeing
that we are surrounded on all hands
with improvements. The plan of "pooh
poohing" an opinion with which we
disagree is an old one, and in many
cases not devoid of advantages;
but magna est veritas et prevalebit
is a still older maxim: and the corollary
is legitimately drawn from the nature
of the premise. As reasonable was the

attempt of the celebrated Mrs Partington to keep out the German Ocean with a mop, as this mode of attempting to stop the progress of Chloroform. If persevered in the same result will follow. The sea will advance and will sweep away those who strive to retard its flow with means so preposterously inadequate. We see even now many signs that the public are getting in advance of the profession upon this subject: and if those members who still object to Chloroform do not take warning in time they will find to their cost that the political world is not the only one where we may witness dethronements.

I propose to pass over the early history of Medicine, altho' it affords ample material for remark: and more especially the quarrels of the 16th Century between the Galenists and the Chemists, for here there was much wrong on both sides.

But coming to more recent times I first notice, as most important, the great discovery of Harvey. Frowned on by those in power, ridiculed by the weak, and pitied by the pseudo great, he pursued his work and perfected it under the cold shade of neglect. For years it was held to be false; he had no encouragement for his labors and he died, with his greatness nearly unacknowledged. But he was a memorable instance of how far one man, serene in suffering as in glory, can go to dignify his kind. In his own time those who favored his views were thought mad. But the man who now denies his greatness and the truth of his theory! Where is he?

Let us look at Jenner and his discovery of vaccination. And while we look let us smile at the rhapsodies of those who opposed him and at the idea that it was a bold defiance of god's holy law. And Mr. Park and Mr. Gre—— join us: ——— is he ——— between the pa—— ph—— Messrs

Park & Bream and those of Massey, Royley & Delafaye. The former on Chloroform, the latter on Vaccination.

Again, regard the improvements introduced into Surgery by Ambrose Paré. The friend of Kings and the Idol of Armies, he could not be neglected or forgotten while he lived: but being dead, one* under Authority tells us the science soon reverted to the state of degradation in which he found it. And as a still more striking circumstance we find that one great innovation which he introduced, the use of the ligature in haemorrhage, had been previously taught and practiced by Celsus and Albucasis; the one 1500, the other 400 years his predecessor.

The discoveries of Sir C. Bell brought out a perfect storm of opposition from all quarters. More than usual violence characterised the opposition to them; and yet who now doubts the apparent sensory endowments of the posterior columns of the spinal cord, or the motory and inherent properties of the anterior?

* Professor Miller.

The history of the introduction of Jesuits bark, whose anti-periodic powers are now probably better established than the virtues of any other article in the materia medica, exhibits along controversy; first as to whether it was good for anything; secondly, why it it acted; thirdly, how it acted; and fourthly, in regard to the mode of exhibition. And is not till its powers were shewn to be absolutely demonstratable facts that it was allowed it's full rights. That is to say — it's merits were admitted when there was no merit in admitting them; but when certain obloquy fell on those who denied their existence.

The stethoscope long languished under the opprobrious name of inutile lignum: Dr. Elliotson was told that he could not diagnose a bit better with than without it: and that if he should be able to do this, he would treat disease no better. The lapse of time has given are clear rope wh. of these opinions. Relt side the ques on whether it becomes professional men to practice in ignorance and in the dark, by mere empiricism, when a light and guide is within their reach.

But I will not extend the list. These instances show sufficiently well the course pursued in all cases of discovery or invention.

Although all people will not agree in considering the light afforded by the history of past events as a beacon for our guidance in the present time and as a prophet to vaticinate for us regarding the shadowy future, it must I think be admitted that all this opposition is of great service in really promoting what it desires to repel. For man is by nature combative and competitive for good or evil: for good most. The discoverer must feel this or his mission can never be successful. Intellect battling with ignorance; energy destroying indolence; mind subduing matter; action, movement

and strength are elements of genius
and necessities of greatness as much
as depth of thought and clearness of
perception. The demigods of the
antique age, the heros of the Grecian
theogony were all competing, combative,
antagonistic intelligences; and wrought
always for man against Hydras, Gorgons
and all savagery. The good they
effected was thought worthy of an apotheosis
and they were lifted into the eternal
heavens of man's heart. The labors of
Hercules and the others should be
regarded as intelligences vanquishing
ignorance; as the teachers and
builders up of the temple of humanity.
When deprived of competition the
world only grows corpulous; when
dumb of ministers, it vociferates with in-
juries. And how wretched the substitute!
The one is intelligence in action, thought
animating matter: in a word it
is antagonism against whatever is
w_____d
Co_____;

coöperation only the subjective, the means whereby the Intelligence affirms itself. The visible agent servant to the invisible power; the organic effects caused by the inorganic forces. The hands are secondary to the head: the indefinite elements must always generate the definite changes; as the thinker the worker, the master the man: for this is the true issue of these two words; and never until these conditions are reversed, until the nerves, arteries and veins change their purposes in mans economy and become superior to his brain, till ponderable matter causates imponderable elements shall the spirit of coöperation rise superior to that of opposition. But though this is the case it forms no justification for the infliction of wrong, or for the opposition to truth, of which I have complained. Seen in its proper light it should only induce us to be thankful that there is a necessity for . . .

which both can and will spread
truth and do good in spite of our
efforts to conceal the one or thwart
the other. In the progress we are
permitted to make we may see
an evidence of the divine goodness
which seems to betoken the perfect-
ibility of our ideas. And in our own
science, in common with others, there
is hope for such a conclusion. For
although we cannot expect soon to
see in it such glorious availments
of the infinite creative power of
nature as we see in some other, yet
we have the high authority of Dr. Alison,
whose name is a guarantee for the
excellence and soundness of the remarks,
for saying, ~~that~~ we may reasonably
hope that the course of time will
bring with it such an augmentation
to our present knowledge that the
prevention or relief of all the
suffering which we now regard as
inseparable, will be

within our power. Is not this a wide and glorious field! And when a man like Dr Alison tells us that such a hope is neither irrational, Utopian, nor inconsistent with past progress, we may, I think, regard the matter as set at rest!

I now proceed to a consideration of the subject to which the title of my thesis is owing. That is, the Religious objections to the use of chloroform in Obstetric Medicine.

Juggernaut, I know, delights in tortures; and Molach, horrid king, besmeared with blood of human sacrifice and parents' tears, is described as taking pleasure in the cries of those suffering pain: yet it appears at first sight absurd to suppose that any one could argue that the Christian Religion, whose only sacrifice is a broken spirit, and whose essence is loving kindness to all men, can be so construed as to refuse us permission to avail ourselves of every means is in our power to alleviation of the ills under which we labour. But it is a widely different thing to study the world as it is and the world as it ought to be: and for all practical purposes of real life we are bound to take the former condition of affairs as the subject of our study. In the present case we find a band of men in, as well as out of your profession declaiming against the use of chloroform in Midwifery because of the interpretation of two words in the 16th verse of the 3rd Chapter of Genesis. Dr Simpson has taken the trouble to trace out the meanings of these words where they occur in other places in the bible, with the view of proving that they do not mean to imply the necessity of physical pain during parturition. But if Dr Simpson considers the form of expression, used in this verse and so frequently elsewhere in the bible, as an imperative sentence and not as a: t: f: I t I believe: I, I do not hold, H . . j a. j . ttle too much. For by proving that their meaning should be rendered "muscular contraction" he has, if, as I said before, he considers the verse a command, debarred himself for ever from the use of turning, the forceps, the air-tractor, the Cesarian section and embryotomy; inasmuch as all these imply the abridgment or abolition of muscular contraction. So that if the verse is read in this way, a woman is to be allowed to die undelivered because she is guilty of the sin of having a contracted pelvis: a sin which is certainly not under her control; and the punishing of which would seem to war with the attributes of infinite wisdom, justice and love, which we regard as the brightest characteristics of the deity.

I do not think that either muscular contraction or physical pain is meant; but simply sorrow, or unhappiness throughout life. My own opinion is that in the form of expression "in sorrow thou shalt bring forth children" the...

command, but a simple prophetic
intimation that woman would never
be perfectly happy: that this is 94 ~
prepared ~~allegorically was~~ allegorically
by saying she should perform her
chief function – parturition – in
sorrow: that is in sorrow of mind. for
it seems unreasonable to suppose we
would be intrusted with the execution
of our own punishment: that a solemn
curse would be pronounced and then
left to depend upon the caprice of the
condemned. But if the meaning
be, as I suppose, sorrow extending
through life, then, do what we will,
the curse remains. In like manner,
man is condemned to eat of the fruit
of the ground in sorrow all the days
of his life. Now if the mere acts of
mastication and deglutition are pointed
at, we neither do not can fulfil the curse.
Nay, what, in this sense, ought to be a curse,
is a positive blessing: for eating, as we
all know, is one of the greatest pleasures
we enjoy. But if it simply mean is that

unhappiness shall be his lot in this
world, then is the curse fulfilled and
not by any possibility to be evaded.

And we are strengthened
in this view if we judge this verse
according to the spirit of Christianity
and according to the revealed
character of its divine Author. Do not
let us believe that our Heavenly
Father desires pain or takes pleasure
in its infliction upon us. Again I
say I know well ~~that~~ the laws of Moloch
require sacrifices to him; and I know
those of Juggernaut involve death
and suffering. But I do not and
cannot believe that the Father of our
Saviour can do other than rejoice
in what saves the sheep of his pasture,
from anguish and from tortures. In
truth I cannot but think that the
entire history of the fall is to be read
allegorically. Under the name of
the serpent who doubts that the devil,
or spirit of Evil is meant? And that
the forbidden fruit was something

widely differing from mere edible
vegetable products. Why then are we
to consider that in one part more is meant
than meets the ear, while we must
read the rest literally? It is admitted
on all hands that God is infinitely just
and true: let us see whether this curse
taken literally is consistent with
justice and truth. It was directed
against Eva and her descendants;
not against the ancestress of a part:
it was addressed to that woman who
was mother of all the nations of the
earth, and to all those who proceeded
from her. Yet we find that in the
Black and in the Aboriginal
American races the sufferings of
parturition are unknown. I am
not aware of any reason why white
women should be more exposed
than blacks to suffer from a curse
pronounced by their common
creator against their common
races. Unless indeed Mr Park and
such as he d'ny that black women

are included in the curse, not being human beings. In this case let these self-styled religious gentlemen look to it. For such an opinion they will find no audience in this country. Or, again, unless they affirm that white and civilised and christian ~~black~~ women are more wicked than their black fellow creatures. This of course is the very antipole of the truth; ~~and~~ but were it the fact, I can discover in the curse no gradation of punishment, according to ~~and wickedness~~ the amount of wickedness. ~~on the other~~ It seems on a par with the other part of the curse which declares that in sorrow shalt thou eat of the ground all the days of thy life. This, it is quite clear cannot be understood literally, from what I said before; and inasmuch as by idiocy or by insanity many are deprived of the power of feeling sorrow. Again it would appear that another part of the curse we are permitted to fulfil by proxy.

the sugar and of the bread and drink of the wine and of the tea which are prepared by the sweat of other peoples' brows. If Mr. Park and those who agree with him, are sincere in their objections, why do they not go and perform their part of the curse to the letter. But such truly cannot fashion to themselves a religion of mercy, and not sacrifice. Then also why should this curse fall so heavily on some, so lightly upon others. Why should one woman perish miserably, after hours of bitter torture; while another shall be a joyful mother, devoid of a single pain; and a third shall never have a child at all. Surely the curse did not ~~mean~~ command that the sins of all should be expiated by the sufferings of a few; even if the sins of the Race could be atoned for by individuals.

Out upon these coldblooded pseudoreligionists, who would call up on us to believe in such contradictions; and a who think we can serve our

Religion and our God by such absence
of feeling, such disgusting inhumanity.
Further, such a reading
would tend to pollute the holy
name by attaching to it the
incompatable terms of just
and cruel, good and sanguinary.
For not only would such a view
of the spirit of the passage do away
with all midwifery for ever, making
it wrong to interfere with the process
in the slightest degree; but it
would do away with all medicine:
seeing that the great end and object
both of medicine & Hygiene is the
prolongation of life; which we
should be forbidden to attempt
by the 19th Verse of the same Chapter, if it is to be read liturally. And
on this subject there is a strange
anomaly with these Anti Chlorofomists.
They do not deny that it may be
an excellent thing in Neuralgia or
in an amputation; but it is not
to be admitted in

most frightful of all pains, in the agonies
of labor. But how inconsistent! If
one part of the curse is to be understood
in this spirit, surely the rest ought
also. To whom is it given that he shall
say of two equal sentences, understand
this one literally; judge that according
to a spirit gathered elsewhere? If we
decide upon one part in this light; then
upon all. And then, we are bound not
to attempt to save men from death.
Now this being the end of medicine, to
admit the force of the curse, is to admit
our Profession to be one map of iniquity;
the practice of it a mockery, a delusion
and a snare. It is to admit that every
particle of animal food we eat is a sin;
that every day in winter and in
Autumn we break the curse by the
absence of sweat upon our brow;
that the Retirement of old age from
active work is contrary to God's law;
that the Senile euthanasia, which
God gives is in ...... to his own
decree; and that every ..... never in a

country farm violates the ~~law~~ sentence by plucking up the thorns and the thistles which the land brings forth: While the unhappy and wicked woman who remains unmarried appears to break the command in four several ways, according to the following tabular statement.

I. She has no conception.

II. She brings forth no children.

III. Her desire is not to her husband.

IV. Her husband does not rule over her.

Now these things certainly form entirely new arguments against Malthusian principles, although they would not, I fear, be admitted as strictly within the rules of reasoning. But are we bound to believe that this verse is to be read literally? I have shewn the unlikelihood of it by the nature of the context. Let us now take a passage or two from other parts of the inspired volume, which may assist us in determining whether we must judge our text to be

part of the bible according to the
spirit or according to the letter.

First, then, let me ask, what
would be the effect were we to
understand litterally the well
known law, "whoso sheddeth man's
blood, by man shall his blood
be shed"? It would abolish venesection
for ever; and as for an amputation!
Of course no surgeon would risk his
own life for the mere purpose of saving
another's.

"A violent man shall not
live out half his days". I know one,
indeed I know several violent men,
who are more than 35 years old:
but I doubt whether I should make
an impartial jury believe me
justified in making away with
them, having no better reason
than this passage.

The days of a man's life are
limited to 70 years, or occasionally
80. But surely no human being,
unless indeed an Antichlor pournist,

would consider on this account that
a man who exceeds the latter age
is unduly and improperly living;
and that another is justified in
destroying him! On the contrary,
our sympathies are all enlisted
in a moment by any outrage
on one of venerable years.

I could multiply these
examples ad infinitum: but these
will show sufficiently well that
the spirit is to be attended to
more than the words, when the
two are discordant: and not
only the spirit of the particular
passage, but the general tenor
of the whole system of Christianity.

It may be said that
these are quoted from men and
that the curse was direct from
God. But the Canons of the Church
admit these writings as of inspired
origin: indeed the whole of your religion
depends upon their force, as derived
by the special grace of God, from

holy men directly inspired by
Him!

To me, I speak with reverence and under correction, the whole
story of the Temptation and of the Fall
appears to be an allegory. We
know the partiality of ancient times,
especially in Eastern Countries, for
the hieroglyphic, or allegorical,
mode of expression: and we find
many instances of it in the Bible.
The one with which we are more
immediately concerned would
seem to express that the perfect
happiness which was the lot of
man till the fall could no more
belong to him and to his Race.
The knowledge of good and of
evil appears chiefly to indicate
that universal feeling of the
existence of an unknown and
unseen world, and of an invisible
power whose anger we deprecate
and whose favour we implore,
by the implanting of a "science"

within us; whereby we are informed
when we are right and when we
are wrong. In the state of innocence
before the fall nothing was thought
of but the light of wrong; one sin
only was within the grasp of those
who dwelt in Paradise. It was
committed; and that its results
implied conscience is proved by
the making of garments and
by the hiding of themselves in the
garden; or rather by whatever
actions *than* typify. This
consciousness, these misgivings, have
existed ever since in all nations,
at all times and in the mind of every
person: for I cannot believe that
any man with his senses entire
disbelieves in the existence of a
superior power, of a great first
cause.

   I am supported in this
opinion by the fact that such an
Idea as that of the Temptation is not
peculiar to the Christian Religion.

The Mexicans have a very old tradition of the same kind, and possess remains of drawings of what they call Cihuacohuati or the Serpent-Woman, whom they also consider to be the mother of Mankind. Humboldt, speaking about this Serpent-Woman, remarks, "these traditions remind us of the old traditions of Asia. In the woman and Serpent of the Aztecks, in Mexico, we think we see the Ivo of the Shemitic nations. In the Ankti cut to pieces, the famous Serpent, Kaliza conquered by Vishnoo, when he assumed the form of Crishna." And the Editor of the People's Dictionary of the Bible says in reference to the same thing, "the whole suggests the idea that the account of the temptation in Genesis is, so to say, the literal translation of a hieroglyphic."

In this opinion I pretty coincide. And this view of the matter

does not present the startling
anomaly of the same being
saving our souls by a gigantic
sacrifice and torturing frail
bodies with unspeakable anguish.
It does not call upon us on the
one hand to regard the grand scheme
of Redemption brought to a point
by the glorious atonement; and on
the other behold a stern sentence
of death and of sorrow, with
the bitter aggravation that powers
are given us to improve our
position and yet that it is wicked
to make use of them. The parable
of the Nobleman and his servants
has been strangely misunderstood
if it signifies that the talent
and abilities God has entrusted
to us are not to be improved;
that they are not to be considered
in the same light as our other
gifts; bestowed upon us that we
may do good and do with them
the work of God and of his Son,

13.

as far as we possibly can. The last emphatic words of the Parable should not be lost on those who oppose action tending in this direction and who would lay claim to the uninterrupted possession of what may be called the vested Rights of Mind. "Unto every one which hath shall be given; and from him that hath not, even that he hath shall be taken away, from him." This is clearly the expression by Christ of the fact that progress and advancement and improvement constitute duties incumbent upon us: while standing still is reprobated and a punishment awarded to it.

I now proceed to notice those pamphlets I have met with which oppose the views I have taken; namely, those of Messrs Gream and Park. for Dr Merriman though considerably [illegible] medical [illegible] [illegible] [illegible] [illegible] in disant

Religion, objections; laying it down
as article that every substance
formed by nature, or which can
be formed by Chemical Manipulations,
is given to man for his use; and
admitting that man has a mind,
capable of considering the properties
of matter. What is to say — for &!
Merriman's distinct Yellow down
will not permit him to speak out —
man has a right to use anything
to increase his pleasure or his pain,
which his mind tells him it
is fit and proper to use — and
in relation to which his conscience
does not interfere to tell him
that its use is opposed to morality,
or to religion.

Were I to search for an
example of the truth of the old french
maxim, Ce n'est que la verité qui
pique, I do not think I could find
a more notable one than in the very
crude and disjointed, angry and
malicious, itt......?

4.

Graam: a Philippic in which the arguments bear the same relation to the *decisan* dogmatic assertions as did Sir John Falstaff's bread did to his sack. A work so constituted it is difficult to pass under review; inasmuch as the salient points which can be animadverted upon are precisely those in which it is most deficient. But, *faute de mieux*, we must take Mr Graam as the chief apposition of the views of those who advocate needless pain in *Restriction*, and remark *seriatim* on his several imaginings. It would be well to arrange these remarks under certain heads; but the ideas *embodied* are so heterogeneous in their nature that such an arrangement is impossible and *I am compelled* to notice them as they appear successively in the *pages of his pamphlet*. The first *section* which ...

Bassanio.   Gratiano speaks an
infinite deal of Nothing, more than
any man in all Venice; his reasons
are as two grains of wheat hid in
two bushels of chaff; You shall
seek all day ere You find them;
and when You have them they are
not worth the search.

to have drawn between natural
and morbid or complicated labor.
This he does partly by an extract
from Denman and partly by his
own remark, "especially during
natural parturition". But can
any thing more grossly
irrational than this be imagined!
Can any one suppose that what is
morally wrong for one form of labor,
is morally right for another, the two
kinds differing only, as regards this
question, in amount of pain? Then,
consider the extreme vanity and
presumption of one thus setting himself up as a judge of when pain
becomes injurious, at what precise
time it is proper to do away with it.
Either pain is an evil or it is not.
If it is an evil as we maintain, then
is it right it should be removed as
soon as possible: if not; then have
we no right to interfere with it in any
degree. If we are to relieve any pain,
surely all.

6.

Physician to prescribe for a case of
chronic Bronchitis, than for one of acute
peritonitis, because the former is
attended with little, the latter with
intense suffering?" In like manner
if Chloroform is to be used at all, let
it not be with the wretched proviso,
that the pain is severe enough: as
though mercy were to be doled out,
like Poor Law relief, and none granted
but under very urgent circumstances.
Ramsbotham Dr Gream.

In reply to the charge that
Chloroform is dangerous in Midwifery
though it is not in Surgery, I answer
that experience, based upon hundreds
of cases, proves, that no danger whatever attends its exhibition; provided
proper care is taken to have the drug
of good quality and to administer it
judiciously. This to be sure is not a
religious objection; but it is an important Medical one and I answer it,
he .... to satisfy .... my
.... I have .... feel it in

seventeen cases of natural labor and I bear witness that while in every instance it entirely freed the patient from pain, in not one was its use accompanied or followed by a single unpleasant symptom. And this I feel assured of, that the deep gratitude of those women for their painless deliveries could not be less acceptable to a merciful God than the horrid shrieks, making night hideous, in which, under like circumstances, others express their sufferings.

It is possible that people carry the tone of their mind into the anæsthetic state, as a pickpocket does his into a church; and so it may be that the woman had her sexual feelings excited as mentioned by Paul Dubois. But Mr Gream forgets that the women of this country are virtuous, are pure minded and are by no means to be compared to Parisian ~~courtesans~~. It might be
courtesans

natural for such a one to be so
excited; but not, therefore, for our
country women. Because the destruction
burned a temple, who will say the
ancient Greeks hated and
persecuted art and destroyed its
works? Because a Paris whore,
unworthy of belief, said her sexual
desires were roused by chloroform,
who will say that pure minded
women can be so affected? Now
this is a serious charge, and it would
be a valid objection were it true. But
fortunately the evidence brought forward
in its favour is derived from a source
entirely worthless; while the testimony
of every one who has used it in Edinburgh
and of most people elsewhere is completely opposed to the existence of
this "revolting influence". My own
experience is altogether in favour
of the latter opinion. Ever since its
discovery I have been daily in the
habit of seeing it administered, or of
administering it myself and I cannot

— Erostratus

too strongly express my utter disbelief
that Chloroform has any such effect.
In truth I regard this change as nothing
more than a piece of special pleading,
and I shall not be ~~tempted~~ surprised
if in his next work Mr Gream tells
us that Chloroform excites the desire to
commit arson or highway robbery.

With the fatal cases asserted
to have taken place from the effects
of chloroform this thesis has nothing
to do. But one cannot help remark-
ing the strong tendency to amal-
gamate the post hoc and the
propter hoc in connexion with
these cases.

The rifacciamento of all
the ~~old women~~ stories propagated
by the old women of ~~nearly~~ both
sexes on the subject of chloroform,
raked up from all quarters, without
particulars or specification of
evidence, ~~that~~ is unworthy arguments
evidence or attention. Not one of the
advocates of Chloroform

50.

the power of preventing death: the
most enthusiastic votary of anaes-
thesia in parturition will readily
agree with Mr Gream that there
are circumstances under which
chloroform cannot with advantage
be employed. But from this fact
we draw no reason for not using
it when it is serviceable. To say it
cannot always be used, is to say
in other words no more than that
it is a medicine. For in the whole
materia medica upon what article
can Mr Gream lay his hand and
say this is not like chloroform; it
can always be exhibited? Upon
Opium? Calomel? Antimony? Quina?
Iron? No not upon one. Then what
does this gentleman mean by ~~an~~
~~ob~~ an objection so entirely childish.
Because he is virtuous shall we
not use our medicines? Were such
an objection considered valid the use of
an in the Pharmacopœia must
be ? en u ... the question

profession would be marvellously
shortened if these peculiarities and
modifying powers of coexistent
circumstances did not exist.
Chloroform is a medicine and it is
to be used as a medicine: not
rashly or indiscriminately, but
with care and caution. It is not
a specific for all the evils of this life:
but it is a valuable step in the
progressive amelioration of our
condition, which seems to be the
most favoured and flourishing object
of divine solicitation: and for my
own part, I differ so totally from Mr
Gream in regard to this agent that
while he looks upon it with distrust,
I am disposed to consider it one of
the choicest ~~and~~ and richest blessings
that has been awarded ~~~~~~~~~~~~
~~~~~~~~~~ to mankind.

The remarks made upon
Mr Gream's pamphlet will for the
most part apply to Mr Park's, his
reasons ~~~~~~~~~~~

identically the same. Fortunately, in this case, they are expressed concisely and intelligibly; twelve pages taking the place of forty four with the best results.

Mr Park is, I understand, a highly respectable and experienced practitioner: he is very evidently an extremely prejudiced one. He seems to have the idea that the means now in our power are quite sufficient for all useful purposes and he appears to deprecate the employment of any new ones. In this spirit he opposes Chloroform and draws a comparison between the use of a wineglassful of Prussic acid and the use of chloroform in labor. This we must treat simply as a case of experience; that is, as Hobbes says, of remembered results, following remembered acts. Now we find that while one is undoubtedly a cause of death in every case, the other is not attended with any danger.

The analogy is absurd; for it is establishing a similarity between the use of a vast overdose in the one instance and of a moderate dose in the other. No one dreams of giving a wineglassful of chloroform at once; and every one, on the other hand — which is the fair analogy — gives Prussic acid in small doses in painful digestion.

Mr. Park argues against a woman's right to evade the appointed penalty. Now I have shewn by parallel passages and otherwise that the form of expression — in sorrow shalt thou bring forth children — is not a command, over which we have control; but simply a prophetic intimation of the divine intention, which will be fulfilled irrespective of human caprice. Moreover, I have shewn that were it a command, it signifies neither pain nor muscular efforts; but simply a life of sorrow, of unhappiness of mind.

Mr Park is extremely pathetic on the voluntary abnegation of consciousness by those who take chloroform. One would fancy, reading his pamphlet, that the world was a pure and sinless calm, that every one in it was patient and enduring, that each moment of every individual's life was well and profitably spent. We know how far otherwise the reality is; and the notion of opposing chloroform on this ground appears most monstrous. And in connexion with this objection he considers there is a difference between the results of opium and of chloroform. But in what this moral difference consists, I am at a loss to conceive. The use of opium in medicine is to relieve pain and to cause slumber: and, in a moral point ~~of~~ of view, of what consequence is the nature of the sleep, provided there are no medical objections. Pain is present in both instances, means are used to relieve it and sleep results.

Every anodyne, calmative and hypnotic in our stores might be objected to on the same grounds. Again it is admitted that six hours daily suffice for all necessary sleep. But how few take less than eight hours. Surely here is a much greater amount of voluntary abnegation of consciousness than Chloroform occasions. Let Mr Park look to this. It offers an extensive field for moral objections.

God, says Mr Park, would have permitted Chloroform to be discovered earlier if it had been proper for us!

Indeed I am quite embarrassed how to answer this objection. The mental blindness, the absence of the simplest reasoning powers, from prejudice, must be so complete in that man's mind, who could chronicle such an opinion, that I despair even by the simplest statement of reaching his understanding. But I will try.

In 1833 Mr

Railway was opened. Mr. Park uses this as a means of travelling; yet, how wicked! A Railway, according to his opinion, is opposed to morality. For if it had been proper for us God would have permitted it to be discovered earlier. Quina, Cod liver oil and Iodide of potassium have not been known many years, yet Mr. Park uses them. Now in his view, they are no better than Chloroform; seeing, if they had been good for us, God would have permitted them to be discovered earlier. If the age in which a thing is discovered is a test of its goodness, why was the Electric telegraph only discovered within this year or two, and not six thousand years ago? Does any one, besides Mr. Park, doubt its utility, or consider it a wicked invention? I tell Mr. Park, that none but himself thinks so; and I say moreover, that however men may doubt it, all things are discovered at the proper period, because appointed by God; that in future time, when a discovery is made he will do wrong to oppose it upon such foolish grounds. Farther, if God would not permit it to be discovered before, being a wicked article, why has he permitted it to be discovered now? I agree that nothing is discovered without God's consent. Chloroform has been discovered and the corollary is obvious.

But this opposition only illustrates what I have said before regarding the progressive nature of all knowledge. It is natural that great blessings should have small attendant evils: and it would, I think, be true philosophy to consider this as in some measure a result of the very curse of which we have spoken. Perfect and unalloyed good is the gift of God alone: we mortals cannot and ought not to expect it. And as reasonable would it be to attack the use of . . . .

Electric Telegraph, because they
have injured mail Coaches, as
to abuse Chloroform for temporarily
abolishing the mental powers.

Both Mr Gream and Mr.
Park pay great attention to the difference
between the occasional, and systematic
use of Chloroform; and between the
amelioration and obliteration of
pain. But one answer will do ~~and~~
for both. What should we think
of the Physician, who, when called
in to a patient in the agonies of a
painful disease should give enough
medicine to relieve a part only and
should still leave a moderate
amount unnoticed and uncared for.
Would such a course be right or
reasonable? Certainly not. If the
great pain is about being, so is the
little pain: if a moderate amount
of pain is a salutary manifestation
of life force*, so is a great amount.

I know not whether Mr Park.
. . . . the

* . . . . .

eleventh page; namely, "because
the Almighty chooses in his wisdom
to act in a certain way, we are not
called upon to do the same." But
I must say a more horrible doctrine
never was broached. Our powers
of doing good must be derived
from God; and being so derived
they must partake of the attributes
of their origin. Every good act
done by Man is only so inasfar as
it is done by the grace of the Holy
Spirit working within him and
urging him to imitate the course
and follow at a vast distance ~~to~~
in the footsteps of the Son of God.

A word more concerning
a passage from the Bible upon which
Mr. Park lays great stress.

Notwithstanding she shall
be saved in childbearing, if they
continue in faith and charity, and
holiness with sobriety.

I say amen to this. Though
I differ somewhat

my reading of it.

For surely God will save by means? Then why may not Chloroform be the answer to the petition? Is it less the gift of God because it did not, as manna in an older time, drop immediately from heaven, but mediately was discovered by the genius God bestowed upon a man?

In my mind's eye I see a woman, the conjugate diameter of whose pelvis measures only three inches; while the smallest diameter of the child's head is three inches and a half. Now in the spirit of Mr. Park's exegesis of the above passage, this poor woman is to be permitted to offer any prayers for her deliverance; but when assistance is tendered in the form of instrumental interference, you are told that if she continue in faith she shall be saved in childbearing: for it, that is the ἡ τεκνογονία and that, an in each a case is a perfect answer to her prayer.

Again I see another in a like situation! Continuing in faith, her prayers are heard. And lo! one appears, bearing in his hand a drug, the gift of God, more potent than opium or mandragora. Then she was laboring in a dread extremity: Now suffering no more than the pleasing punishment that women bear.

I discover myself as one having a poor opinion of Mt. Park's exegitical powers.

"It shaweth an exceedingly great pride and rashness in Machiavell that he dare speake and write of the affaires of warre and prescribe precepts and rules unto them which are of that profession, saying hee had nothing but by heare-say: and was himselfe but a simple Secretarie, or Town Clarke, which is a trade as different from

the profession of warre, as one
harquebush differs from one pen
and inkhorn. Herein it fals
out to Machiavell, as it did mee
to the philosopher Phormio; who
one day reading in the
Peripatetike schoole of Greece,
and seeing arrive and enter thither
Annibal of Carthage (brought
by some of his friends to hear the
eloquence of the Philosopher) hee
began to speake and to dispute
(with much babbling) of the laws
of warre and of the duties of a
great Captaine, before this
most famous Captaine which
had forgotten more than that
philosopher ever knew or had
learned. Now when hee had
ended his lecture and goodly
disputation, as Annibal went
from the auditorie one of his
friends, which had brought him
thither, demanded what hee thought
of the philosopher's eloquence and

gallant speeche? To whom
Annibal replyed: Truly I have
in my lifetime seene many
elderly females, but I never saw
so old a woman as this Phormio."

I have and my thesis.
I have discussed the general principles
of the case and their special application.
The subject is an important one; inasmuch as it involves a charge of
quackery and irreligion against
many members of my profession.
The choice of a subject for
a thesis is a difficult one; and I rejoice
to think that the one I have selected
will atone for the defects of the Author.
I feel a great satisfaction
in thinking that & ultimately truth
must prevail: it is derived from
God and shares his attribute of
immortality. Other things may
come and go but truth is ever
advancing! Upon this man's
banner is written a word ... or,

and his Course is still upward
and upward. The feeling of self-
reliance, so necessary for self-
development, is spreading; the highly
wrought antagonism of the present
age is favorable to our progress; man
is becoming acquainted with his
destiny and ~~labors~~ strives more to perform
his duty; He has done much and
eminent results have followed from
his labors.

All things confess his strength; through the cold mass
Of marble and of color his dreams pass;
Bright threads whence mothers weave the robes
                    their children wear:
Language is a perpetual orphic song;
Which rules with dædal harmony the throng
Of thoughts, and forms, which else senseless
                    and shapeless were:
The lightning is his slave; Heaven's utmost deep
Gives up her stars, and, like a flock of sheep,
They pass before his eyes, are numbered
                    and roll on:
The ... fest is ... the air;
An ... ... of the ... bare,

Heaven! hast thou secrets? Man unveils me:
I have none.

That all the world had a true sense of the giant power for good and for evil with which we are endowed. For then would justice and truth prevail and the desire to do good and to discover truth animate every breast: then would the fulfilment of our creator's spirit, as far as mortals can carry out the spirit of the Eternal, be the exceptionless rule throughout the land's length and breadth. Heaven speed the day when all shall do this in sincerity and in disinterestedness. Meanwhile may the sneers they deserve be the lot of those who even now are engaged in the good work.

Soon after the discovery of
Chloroform I wrote to my father upon the
subject of the religious objections, and
in reply received from him the
following letter. Coming from one
of consummate learning, of real
powers of mind and a constant student
of the Bible I regard it as of great
importance. Indeed if the opinion
of men, who are competent to judge,
received proper attention, Dr Chalmers'
remark about the small theologians
in the ~~poisoning~~ this letter ought to settle
the matter. Especially when opposed
only by men, who, alike by mental
qualifications, by education and by
pursuits, are unfitted for expressing an
opinion upon such a subject.

December, 1847.

My dear Francis,

Lay this fact to your
heart, whether a great fact, a middle
sized fact or a little fact I know not, but
of ... it ... true ... d ... a
... a ... a ... t the ... in of

Muscat and sending a letter to Your Shoemaker in George Street Edinburgh, the
difference, as to trouble of body, as to anxiety
of mind and indeed as to postage is
next door to Nothing. The Shoemaker,
it is true, receives Your letter, if once
it is lodged in the post office, without
farther trouble on Your part. But so does
His Highness of Muscat. The true point of
difficulty is — (and in that stage of the
transaction the Shoemaker costs You quite
as much trouble as the Imaum) first of
all to reach the post office. Hic labor,
Hoc Opus est. And for us especially it is
So. The interval remember between us
and this particular post office at Lepwade.
(meaning by interval the total diaulos
of to and fro, outward and homeward
voyages) is a good three miles.
Hence my delay and also from this
other Cause; that having mislaid
your jotting of doubts and queries, I had
lost the only guide to my own replies
and suggestions.
I. As to ...

dramatic poet Middleton, I feel satisfied (from the internal evidence) that it is genuine. The only demur connects itself with the date – 1654 – (If you are right in reporting that as the date it puzzles me.) What motive or encouragement could a publisher have for bringing out any Book connected with the stage between 1640 and 1660? Cromwell died in 1658 and certainly the period of his Protectorate was not the gloomiest of that puritanical Vicennium, but it was gloomy enough. There was no motive of gain at that time, and there might be some dangers in publishing what were viewed as wicked books by the dominant party.

II. But why should there be any difficulty as to Middleton's having noticed a fact which Dr. Simpson, I think, shews, (but here I am speaking from memory) to have been known

Medicine was much attended to
by the literary men of the 17th
Century: for instance the use of
<u>friction</u>, the application of the
<u>metallic tractors</u>, as practised 40
or 50 years ago by the American
empiric — all this was elaborately
anticipated by Greatrex in
Charles II d's reign. He again had
certainly been anticipated by
Greeks and Romans. Somewhere
in Plautus, I remember a jesting
allusion to the medical treatment
by traction, in which allusion the
adverb <u>tractim</u> seems as part
of the expression. And subsequently
I remember to have met with
cryptical allusions to most of the
<u>medical raving</u>, which we
regard as most peculiarly of
modern growth, in Greek writers
before the 6th Century of our æra.
I must also have pointed out to you
the still more singular fact that
Hahnemann's doctrines, not as to

infinitesimal doses but) as to Homœ
apathy and Allœopathy is most
distinctly stated and ably exemplified
by Milton about 1641 – viz: in the
preface to his Samson Agonistes. It
is clear that Milton had reflected
deeply on Physiology, and other
branches of your splendid and
infinite profession.

Any reader of this assertion
will naturally be startled even more
by the situation of such a strange
hypothesis, than by its authorship –
but its local connexion with a
Hebrew tragedy, than by its personal
connexion with Milton. Strange
enough in all conscience, that a
great poet of the 17th Century should
anticipate the German medical
innovator of the 19th Century; but
stranger still, that for a medical
or physiological hypothesis, this
great poet should have devised no
more suitable situation than in a
critical disputation on the principles

of Art, concerned in the Greek tragic
drama. So it is however; and really
the Miltonic Hahnemannism is
more satisfactory than the Miltonic
criticism on Grecian Art. Those difficult
questions that arise upon the Greek
ideas of tragedy are but grazed or
ruffled upon the surface. True—there
was not room for doing much more—
But then the room was even less
that was ~~disposeable~~ disposeable
for Hahnemann—and yet in the
very few words uttered, a most
comprehensive outline of the doctrine
is sketched, which scarcely allows
of improvement. Neither is the
introduction of this medical digression,
after all, so violent an intrusion as
one imagines before hand. It arises
naturally enough upon the well known
but obscure passage in Aristotle,
ascribing to tragedy the office of
purifying the passions by ministration
of pity and terror. The first demur
of any note upon this passage is—

"How? — purify a passion by a passion?"
"Why yes — even so!" is virtually Milton's
reply. It seems a strange rationale
of medical practice; but in effect it
is the very logic nature prompts us
to, in the treatment of our own bodily
morbid affections. For in a diarrhœa
we do not proceed by introducing
a counter agency, but a similar
agency. We do not curb the diarrhœa:
on the contrary we ~~mimic~~
mimic the natural diarrhœa by
an artificial diarrhœa through
medicine. Again if a man suffers
from a morbid discharge of blood,
is it the policy of medicine violently
to restrain that discharge? Far
from it. The first step is to bleed
the patient. The morbid hæm—
orrhage is attacked by an artificial
hæmorrhage which often succeeds
in re-establishing the disordered
system. That is to say rather or
it, — it affections are redressed
by similar affections

and not by _alloia pathē_, affections
of an alien nature.

What strange vagaries
does literature present! Strange
almost as those of nature.

Now, as regards the
monstrous objections, calling themselves
religions, to Dr Simpson's immortal
discovery (which discovery I should
think will be found to have done
more for human comfort, and for
the mitigation of animal suffering,
than any other discovery whatever!).
the Doctor's own arguments seem
quite sufficient. In the same
spirit as these arguments might
be suggested such as the following.
I. "Three score years and ten":
This is the limit assigned to human
life in the Psalms. Consequently in
the logical of these "religious"
Cavillers, it must be impious to
prescribe for a man of 80. And the
whole science of Macrobiotics must
rank with witchcraft.   xuey

in point of wickedness. Lord Bacon thought otherwise.

II. "Poverty shall never cease from the land": Ergo it must be profane to attempt the limitation of poverty; and absolutely blasphemous to effect its extirpation, as was once done in the New England States and elsewhere.

III. "In sorrow shalt thou bring forth." Dr. Simpson's improved interpretation of the Hebrew word, making it to indicate the muscular uterine exertion which attends parturition, (and attends it so pre-eminently in the human female) rather than to indicate the pain generally connected with this exertion, seems quite sufficient for the occasion. Another argument suggests itself: viz: that if all pain when carried to the stage which we call agony (or intense struggle amongst vital functions) brings with it some danger to life (a................ it be the case) then it.............. at.......... ly to

reject a means of mitigating, or
wholly cancelling the danger, now
that such a means has been discovered
and tested, travels on the road towards suicide. If I am right in
supposing a danger to life, lying in
this direction, then clearly the act
of rejecting the remedy, being wilful,
lies in a suicidal direction. It is
even worse than an ordinary movement in that direction; because it
makes God an accomplice, through
the Scriptures, in this suicidal
movement; nay the primal insti-
gator to it by means of a supposed
Curse interdicting the use of any
means whatever (though revealed
by Himself) for annulling that Curse.
This turns the tables on the
religiosity people; landing them
in the guilt of abetting what will
be henceforward be regarded as
a step towards suicide — viz: by
abetting the rejection of a known
anodyne, potent enough to disarm

the chances of a fatal issue.

IV. On the argument which would forbid the use of this almost magical anodyne, all the prophylactic means hitherto used for lessening the violence of symptoms in parturition, must have been lawful only in the inverse ratio of their efficacy. To be altogether clear of guilt, the means used must be confessedly and altogether ineffective. I do not pretend to any knowledge upon this subject — but I have a general impression that bleeding and other means are employed in long stages antecedent to child birth, for the purpose of disarming the symptoms before hand of their violence, and preparing an easier course of gestation, as well as an easier delivery. Now, if so, what wretches these practitioners must suddenly discover themselves to have been! Do they fancy that if ⋯ ⋯ ⋯ ⋯ offence to disarm

a sting partially and before hand,
how that newly discovered offence
of plucking out the sting completely,
at the moment of its hostile action?!
Is their only excuse for this long series
of crime, that after all, their work was
done imperfectly? That they failed
to give relief — is that their plea?
My advice to these villains is — to
remember the old argument "In
for a penny, in for a pound": they
are already up to the lips in
guilt: let them therefore like
sensible reprobates, go the whole
hog by patronising Chloroform.
V. There is a case parallel to this
in the popish Codes of casuistry.
Is it not a scriptural doctrine that
we should mortify the flesh?
Certainly it is. No Protestant denies
it. And upon that argument many
a young woman in Convents, with
the sanction of her directors and
Confessors, has founded a reputation
for saintliness upon the practice

of swallowing the most revolting
selections of filth. Southey illustrated
a shocking case of that nature in
the Quarterly Review. But in the
Dublin newspapers, and I think
about the same time, occurred a
case of the same kind, that
terminated in consequences, over
which no veils of cloister secrecy
could be drawn. A young girl,
under some popish superstition,
ate large quantities of the earth
around the grave of some Priest
who had died in the odor of
sanctity. This odor, meantime,
had not availed to banish the
larvæ of some hideous beetles. These
established themselves in the poor
girls intestines. A dreadful illness
ensued with what final result
I do not remember. How this mode
of mortifying the flesh by positive
acts; viz: by eating vermin,
his influence p as nt a thie hlouform
n in itifging th flesh by

negative acts – viz:, by abstaining
from chloroform, in the final consequences:
both modes augment the chance of
death, and therefore load with the
guilt of suicide those who knowingly
become parties to either. The two
practices are akin also in this –
that both have drawn a furious
support from superstition – both
plead scriptural words for practices
that are essentially unscriptural.
VI. Dr. Simpson's notice of the exemption
from the worst sufferings of childbirth enjoyed by some races of
women is much strengthened by
various Polynesian experiences.
Of any that Ellis notices these
cases in his Polynesian Researches.
In a separate work (not by Ellis) on
the particular island of Tonga (i.e.
Tonga taboo, or Tonga the sacred)
I remember a case of total immun-
ity from pain or even momentary
lassitude in a native woman
during parturition.

VII. Now, addressing myself no longer to everybody, but to you, in particular, I am of opinion that your own exegesis or suggestion for another exegesis of the original curse — is plausible, and will be thought so by Dr. Simpson. to VI argues that the curse is not unconditional, but is perhaps dependant on conditions of diet, of habits engrafted on civilization &c. Once removed the curse loses its sanctity. Dr. Simpson again by his new ~~version~~ version of ~~the~~ Hebrew word, so transmutes the whole bearings of the passage, as to ~~connect~~ disconnect it from all liability to these religious scruples against Chloroform in Childbirth: nothing is disturbed by the Chloroform that ever was fixed by the primal decree. Next, comes your own suggestion, which while retaining the curse, evades it by a new interpretation. If it were said ... ... eat thy bread"

we should not understand the
sorrow as settling upon the act
of taking food, which on the
contrary is one of the commonest
enjoyments of life; but we should
understand that life itself as a
general function of the body, was
described by one of its most general
necessities. So also in this case
you understand the curse addressed
to woman; being simply that she,
not less than her partner man,
should sorrow through life. But
life in her is described by a
variation of phrase suited to her
sexual differences. In man it had
been expressed by his peculiar and
separate form of activity; viz: by
labor applied to the creation of food.
In woman the characteristic and
differential form of activity being
applied — not to the gaining of a
livelihood — but to the necessities,
cares, innumerable duties connected
with the bringing into the world and

the rearing of children, the expression of the curse has varied itself corres- pondingly. The two modes of expression vary with the Sex: but the thing expressed is exactly the same; viz: the whole tenor of life; denoted in each by the function which lies upon the surface and strikes the understanding as most distinguishing. It might have been said, with the same exact meaning — "man, Thou shalt plough the ground in sorrow:" — to woman, Thou shalt spin the gar- ments of thy household in sorrow": but the Scriptural expression has settled upon still wider forms for indicating most comprehensively the process of life. The Curse there- fore is by you to read as to extend itself to life generally; and not as limiting itself to the Sources of Sorrow involved in the production of Children. But lastly if the curse were so limited; I say, if the Curse be so understood as limited to the

evils arising through maternity, why
should those evils be contemplated as
lying chiefly in the very ~~transitory~~
transient and physical act of
parturition? Agonizing as the sufferings
from childbirth have occasionally
proved (as many great obstetric surgeons
have assured us), expressing their fury
sometimes by sudden lunacy the
most frantic, sometimes by infanticide
unconscious or semi conscious ——
Consequences that henceforth are
doomed to subside as the billows of
the tormented Red Sea before the
uplifted rod of Amram's son, ——
still these sufferings are transitory
as compared with the life long
fears, cares, and trepidations
connected with the rearing
training, and disposal of children.
There lies the sorrow; there the
opening for a real curse; viz: in
the moral and not in the mere
physical woe; in the moral woe
that last time in the second

not in the physical woe that after
a few days' fearful heaving and
convulsion is hushed into a deep rest
from the storm — either that rest
which lies in restoration to health,
or in the deeper rest which lies
in the sabbath of Death.

VIII. If it were possible that, in this
age of the world, religious scruples
such as those now passed in review
could maintain their ground, it is
certain that a conflict absolutely
without precedent and shocking to
contemplate, would arise between
the scrupulous practitioner and
his patients. A general knowledge
of the new anodyne, and of its
instantaneous efficacy will be
diffused with a rapidity correspond-
ing to the extensive field of its
application. The whole female
sex have within a few weeks come
into possession of a great inheritance,
of a boon which all duty is it very
near ___ to them; and the views of

His talisman apply themselves
to the very class of cases, that naturally
besiege the terrified imaginations
of females beyond all others. A
new anchor has been made known,
fitted for the special order of storms
that are the most widely appalling
to females, as being the Catholic
inheritance of their sex. This they
will now demand when suffering
in extremity. To refuse would be—
to create scenes the most dreadful
of feud between the medical
attendant and his patients. The
issue of such feuds could not be
long doubtful. But in the meantime
they would create a scandal
shocking to a profession of gentlemen.
IX. And finally, is there any real
religious scruple at the bottom of
these objections? Is it not a jealousy
of Professor Simpson's great discovery
that really speaks through this
jesuitical masquerade of conscientious
scruples?　　Thomas de Quincey.

CPSIA information can be obtained at www.ICGtesting.com
Printed in the USA
LVOW112159080713

341897LV00016B/561/P